Children of the World
Paint Jerusalem

Children of the World
Paint Jerusalem

Forewords by Danny Kaye and Teddy Kollek, Mayor of Jerusalem

Introduction by Ayala Gordon, Curator, Youth Wing, Israel Museum, Jerusalem

BANTAM BOOKS · TORONTO · NEW YORK · LONDON

CHILDREN OF THE WORLD
PAINT JERUSALEM

*A Bantam Book / published by arrangement with
Keter Publishing House Jerusalem Ltd.*

PRINTING HISTORY
Keter edition published June 1978
Bantam edition / October 1978

*The paintings in this book are from the exhibition "Children of the World Paint
Jerusalem," organized by Israel's Central Office of Information in cooperation
with the Israel Museum, the Municipality of Jerusalem, the Ministry for Foreign
Affairs, the Ministry of Tourism, El Al Israel Airlines and Bank Leumi Le-Israel.*

ISBN 0-553-01114-6

Published simultaneously in the United States and Canada

*Bantam Books are published by Bantam Books, Inc.
Its trademark, consisting of the words "Bantam Books" and
the portrayal of a bantam is registered in the United States
Patent Office and in other countries. Marca Registrada.
Bantam Books, Inc., 666 Fifth Avenue, New York, New York 10019.*

Printed and bound in Italy by Staderini

0 9 8 7 6 5 4 3 2 1

Jerusalem, Israel's capital, presents many faces: the Old City and the New, everyday Jerusalem and the Jerusalem of hope and prayer, Jerusalem of today and that of the past.

When we first suggested to the children of the world that they paint Jerusalem, we expected to receive 20,000 paintings. To our surprise and delight, 150,000 children responded.

Children from Japan and Venezuela, from Korea and Switzerland, from America and South Africa, envisioned a city they had never seen. Each child drew the city as he imagined it. Each saw Jerusalem as his own.

Our daily task in reunited Jerusalem is to make it truly a city of peace. Thus we were pleased to see that many of the drawings reflected the children's view of Jerusalem as a city of brotherhood and peace.

For us, this is a sign of hope.

Teddy Kollek

Teddy Kollek,
Mayor of Jerusalem

Foreword by Danny Kaye

Children the world over, with a few heartbreaking exceptions, are full of hopes and dreams. Their fertile imaginations and innocence, their capacity for joy and total lack of hypocrisy have always given me present pleasure and hope for the future.

To me, children are very special people, and Jerusalem, the subject of this book, a very special place. Jerusalem the legendary, Jerusalem the golden; the goal, the center, the shrine of three of the world's major religions. Ever since it was stormed and taken by King David in 1000 B.C., the city has inspired painters, poets, prophets, and pilgrims, not to forget the philosophers and politicians with their visions of peace and dreams of empire. Now, in this unique book, Jerusalem is the inspiration for paintings by children from forty-three countries. Children and Jerusalem—what a delightful and original combination!

As I looked at the paintings I saw a hundred mirrors in which the universal dream of Jerusalem is reflected in wonderfully creative, colorful, and meaningful art. Naturally, the concepts and styles are as varied as the experiences and environments of the children. Cherry trees blossom in Jerusalem in the painting of a Japanese boy; there are Jerusalems inhabited by American Indians, Mexican farmers and Renaissance madonnas; Jerusalems with landscapes that call to mind Tahiti, and Africa, old Vienna and the Baghdad of *A Thousand and One Nights*.

One cannot fail to be impressed by the artists' sincerity and optimism, their joy and faith, and by the dreams of peace and fellowship that are the underlying message of these paintings. Witness one in which an Argentine girl winningly depicts a dream of herself as a beauty queen, showering her beauty of spirit and largesse in the form of hearts over the Holy City, and a valentine to peace by twelve-year-old Avigal Matalon of Israel which expresses the universal dream of Jerusalem united.

As UNICEF's official ambassador-at-large to the children of the world, it is with pride and affection that I congratulate all the contest winners, and thank all the talented young people who submitted their paintings.

I wonder, are these the little children who will lead us?

I hope so.

Introduction by Ayala Gordon
Curator, Youth Wing, Israel Museum, Jerusalem

In November 1976, as part of the tenth anniversary of the reunification of Jerusalem, Mayor Teddy Kollek wrote a *Letter to the Children of the World*, inviting them to paint the Holy City and compete for the winning prize of a week's stay in Israel.

The competition, limited to children between the ages of 7 and 14, was organized by Israel's Central Office of Information, the Municipality of Jerusalem, in cooperation with the Ministry for Foreign Affairs, the Ministry of Tourism, the Israel Museum, El Al Israel Airlines, and Bank Leumi Le-Israel.

Schools, art centers, and museum classes were approached in almost all countries around the globe. The contest evoked an enthusiastic response, astonishing in volume. Some countries even organized their own exhibitions before sending the entries to Israel. The Guayasamin Museum of Ecuador, for example, held an impressive show, complete with posters and a catalogue.

All told, more than 150,000 paintings were received from forty-three nations. It took almost a month for the judges to narrow down the entries to 400 paintings, which were then exhibited at the Israel Museum in Jerusalem. The exhibition drew enormous crowds of both adults and children who found themselves deeply moved and amused by the work of the young artists.

In September 1977, the thirteen contest winners from other countries spent a week in Israel. They toured the country and spent an entire day at the Museum, painting with Israel's children at the Youth Wing studios. At the ceremony awarding the prizes, a little kimono-clad winner from Japan performed a cherry blossom dance, to the delight of all.

Some 110 of the paintings that were exhibited at the Israel Museum appear on the following pages. We have tried our best to distinguish the signatures which the children appended to their work, but since not all of them were clear, we apologize for any unavoidable inaccuracies.

The criteria used in selecting the paintings were the following: Relevance to the theme, sincerity and application in the execution, originality in interpretation, power of expression, and decorative qualities.

We tried to select those works which were truly the product of children and typical of their age group. This was complicated at times when the child was exceptionally talented or had received highly sophisticated art training.

The themes that had been suggested for the competition included "Jerusalem the Golden," "The Holy City," "City of the Spirit," "City of Peace," and "I Am in Jerusalem." All these were represented in the entries, but the interpretations were quite varied. The majority of the paintings depicted the landscape of the city itself, both old and new, as interpreted by the child, either realistically or imaginatively. There were, however, a number of variations, including celestial Jerusalem, Jerusalem as the center of the world, and the Holy City of the three monotheistic religions. Children in the Catholic countries tended to show the city as a concept rather than a geographic location, some happily placing the Sea of Galilee or Bethlehem within the city limits.

The children tended to interpret Jerusalem in the light of their own experience, often producing amusing results. A Swiss boy, for instance, imagined Jerusalem in a setting of mountains with a cable car added for good measure. Others had real information included in their paintings. Bobo from Burma included representations of Ben-Gurion, Teddy Kollek, a beauty queen, and Karl Marx in his five entries. Pablo of Venezuela portrayed Moshe Dayan, Moses, and, also, a beauty queen in his drawings.

It was intriguing to discover a whole range of stylistic and perceptual influences of adult art on that of the children—a Mexican madonna reflects folk art, the Belgian landscape reminds us of the Flemish Old Masters, an Austrian landscape brings to mind medieval manuscripts, and many others are reminiscent of children's book illustrations.

The Madonna and Child, the Crucifixion, and hosts of heavenly angels were particularly prominent in paintings from Catholic countries. An especially expressive Crucifixion was painted by a six-year-old from Ecuador, while a group from Sweden painted the Crucifixion flanked by Israeli flags and angels. In a number of landscapes from Sweden, compositions suggesting crosses were created, quite possibly without the children being aware of the fact.

Similarly, Jewish themes, such as praying, dancing, or crying near the Western Wall, were common. Some were very expressive, while in others the interpretation was strange and the Wall clearly an enigma to the child. A Japanese child drew the Wall with Japanese crying and hugging each other next to it, and the leader of the Makoya sect floating in a halo above it.

Symbolic interpretations were, at times, very curious and intriguing. One painting showed a Zeus-like god hovering in the sky over a strange bug, in the form of a walled city. A Jewish boy from Holland and a Japanese child painted just eyes. One child showed Jerusalem reflected in the tears dropping from two eyes, while the Japanese boy painted two crosses reflected in a pair of eyeglasses. Other symbolism was more direct. An Israeli child and a German girl expressed love of Jerusalem by painting the city in the shape of a heart.

Occasionally there were exceptional talents, though originality was relatively rare. We were surprised to learn that among the few works selected there were, in a number of cases, separate paintings by siblings, supporting the notion that talent runs in families.

For the many thousands of children who participated, the most important aspect was not the "competition" but the fact that they learned about Jerusalem. Adults looking through this book, or those who saw the exhibition of the paintings, will be impressed by the profound symbolic and emotional significance of Jerusalem to people the world over, as expressed by the works of the children.

These examples of children's art also give us an idea of the level of art education in some forty countries throughout the world. Those of us who participated in the selection of the paintings saw whole groups, usually the work of a single class, which were homogenous—either very well executed or very poorly done. Clearly the children depended heavily on their art teacher both in terms of preparatory information, motivation, and technical guidance.

We were able to gather more information about the Israeli children by means of questionnaires. One girl explained that "I had never visited Jerusalem, so I thought, let me imagine how it looks and paint it with beautiful colors." Since her work bore a strong resemblance to the other paintings produced by her class it seems likely that the teacher suggested most of the ideas. However, the child had absorbed these ideas and was convinced that they were her own. This is probably true of many of the paintings, which thus reflect both adult and child values.

All of these paintings reflect the physical environment and cultural values of the children who painted them. They also mirror the place and meaning which Jerusalem occupies in the minds and hearts of people around the world. The profound impression that they leave on us is due to the sincerity, seriousness, and naiveté of the children who painted them, as well as to their power of expression. Perhaps this is the reason that they move us much more than similar paintings by adults.

When we asked the Israeli children how they would like to spend a day at the Museum, the answer was almost always the same: "I want to see the paintings of the other children, but mainly I want to meet the other children and get to know them."

Perhaps this is also the message of this book—becoming acquainted with a hundred children from many countries through their paintings.

The work of the thirteen contest winners from around the world, plus four winning entries by Israeli children, are designated throughout the book by a dot. ●

Angelo Sacedoti, Italy

Pablo Antonio Martinez, age 10, Venezuela

Orlando Virgilio Ampudia, age 10, Ecuador

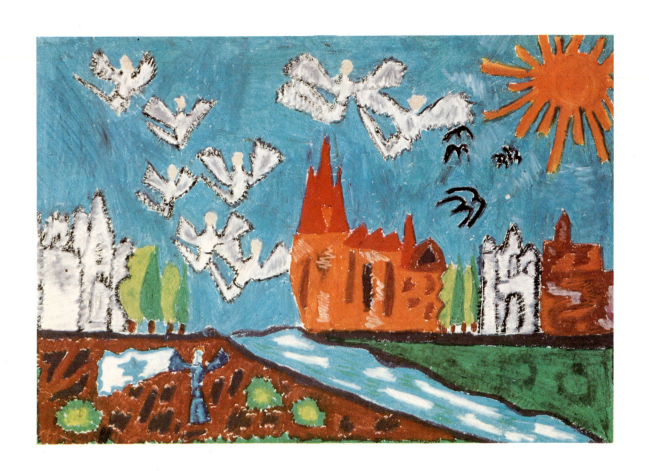

Zippy Byaly, age 13, Israel

Warren Hawkins, age 11, U.S.A.

Marie Eckerlid, age 12, Sweden   Group Work, age 13-14, France

Alexandra Winocur, age 7, Israel

Reimar Wirr, age 12, West Germany

Amos Chedyera, age 12, Malawi

Adam Jroman, age 11, Canada

Group Work (Herzlia School, Capetown), age 9-11, South Africa

Avigail Matalon, age 12, Israel

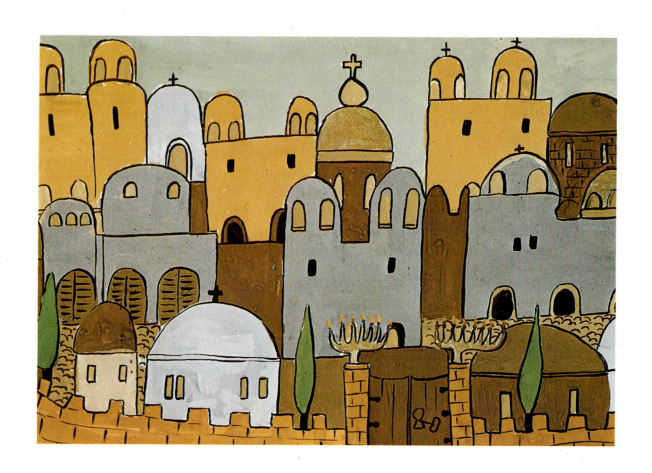

Helene D'Alteroche, age 11, France

Dieter Stucky, age 8½, Switzerland

Dueb El-Duek, age 11, Israel

● Genevieve Meissonnier, age 11, France

Matsuyo Taniuchi, age 10, Japan

Martha Mariana Castro Flores, age 10, Mexico

Norbert Gringel, age 8, West Germany

Odile Dubouloz, age 9, France

Dudi Gershon, age 11½, Israel

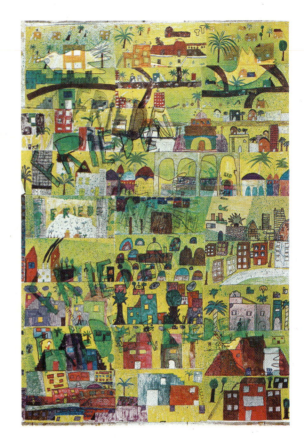

Catherine Pavia, age 9½, France

Group Work, age 9, West Germany

Iris Havusha, age 12½, Israel   Philippe Irazoqui, age 12, France

Jay Cross, age 14, Cyprus

● Shmulik Dudai, age 11½, Israel

Gabriele Skala, age 9, Austria

Barbara Hillman, age 12, West Germany

Claire-Marie Cloquet, age 14, Belgium

Veronique Farinelle, age 13, Belgium

De Tempel

Jolien van der Heide, age 9, Holland

● Dafnit Wiener, age 13½, U.S.A.

● Nitzana Breda, age 11½, Israel

Elisabeth Fritz, age 12, France

● Alexandro Ley Hermandez, age 8, Mexico

Ofer Aptowitzer, age 10, Israel

Beatrice Weder, age 11, Guatemala

Kwon Mee Ryung, age 9, South Korea   ● Em Kyong Chon, age 9, South Korea

Adel El-Duek, age 11, Israel

Bianca Marcella, age 14, Italy

Camilla Jonsson, age 12, Sweden

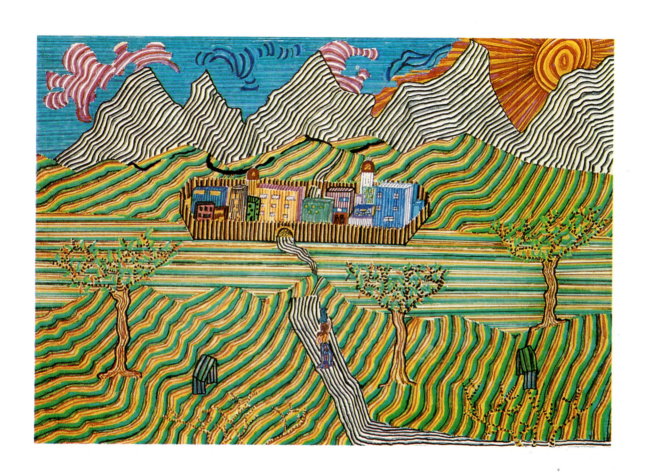

Deborah Terracina, age 13, Italy

Yakobe Ngulube, age 14, Malawi

Enrico Acquadro, age 12, Italy

• Chana Shitrit, age 11½, Israël

Kent Mattsson, age 11, Sweden

Sabine Kaufmann, age 10, Austria

Fabienne Astier, age 12, France

Batia Brener, Uruguay

Nadia Roustin, age 12, France

Ana Lorenza Malare, age 12, Venezuela

Franjo Tunjic, age 8, Austria

Bruno Bernard, age 10, France

Jay Dickens, age 11, U.S.A.

Jannie van Bruggen, age 12, Holland

Kristina Loegren, age 9, Sweden

Monica Rostan, age 11, Italy

Segundo Juan Vaca Diaz, age 15, Ecuador

Thomas Redl, age 10, Kenya

Renate Weber, age 12, Austria

Boaz Herman, age 10, Israel

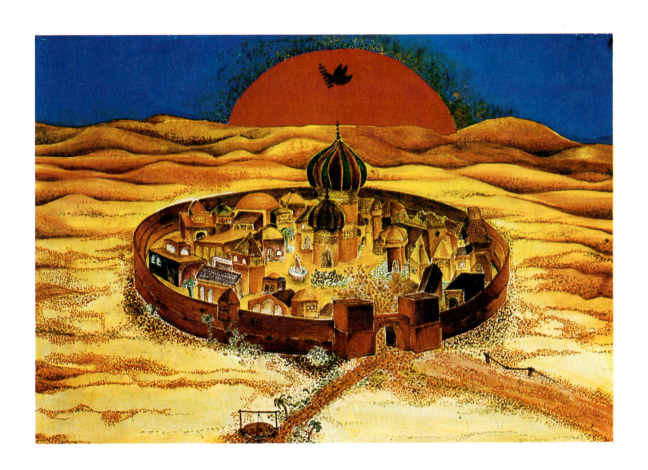

● Koen de Smet, age 13, Belgium

David Bolling, age 13, Sri-Lanka

Shai Mogilner, age 8½, Israel

● Leigh Robinson, age 9, South Africa   Patricia Lorena Ramirez Rayez, age 11, El-Salvador

Gilda Josefina Mariotti Fernandez, age 14, Paraguay

Hirosumi Mitiko, age 9, Japan

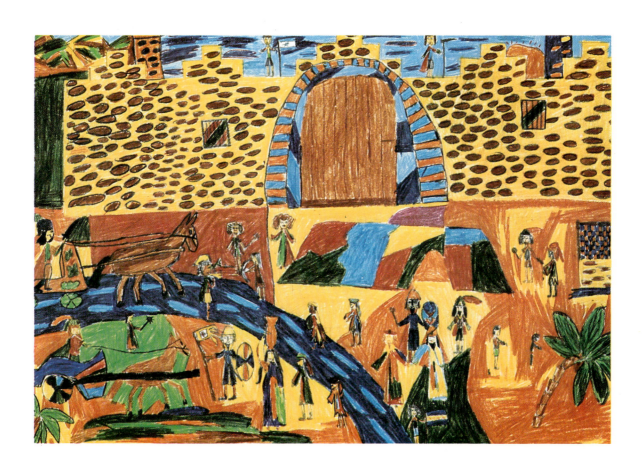

Judith Haasnoot, age 10, Holland

ירושלים של זהב

Tami Nettler, age 11½, Israel

Marie Iatchenko, age 14, France

Debora Weisvein, age 13, Argentina

Peter Schadde van Dooren, age 10, Holland

Anna Katharin Palden, age 13, Austria

Jerusalem, la Ciudad Santa.

Sergio Rodriguez Medina, Mexico

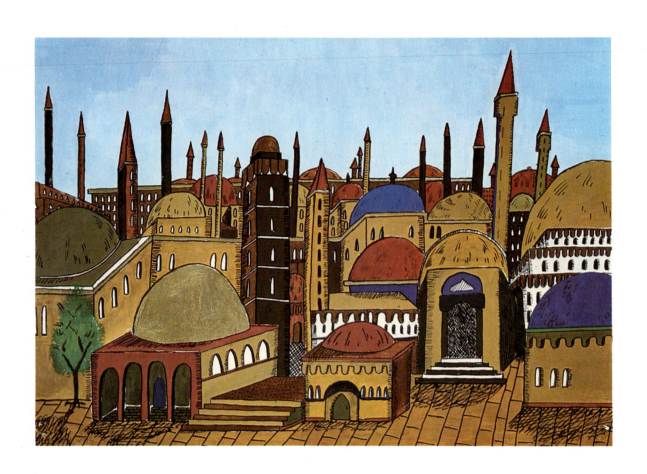

Massimo Gotti, age 13, Italy

Yern Kyung-Sook, South Korea

Pernilla Balkhag, age 12, Sweden

Thomas Osterwalder age 13, Switzerland

Group Work, age 9, Holland

Leonhard Christian Palden, age 9, Austria

Caterina Robba, Italy

Noleen Venter, age 7, Malawi

Mariana Sammartino, age 10, Argentina   Carol Elizabeth Gedance, age 14, El-Salvador

● Sophie-Elisabeth Palden, age 10, Austria

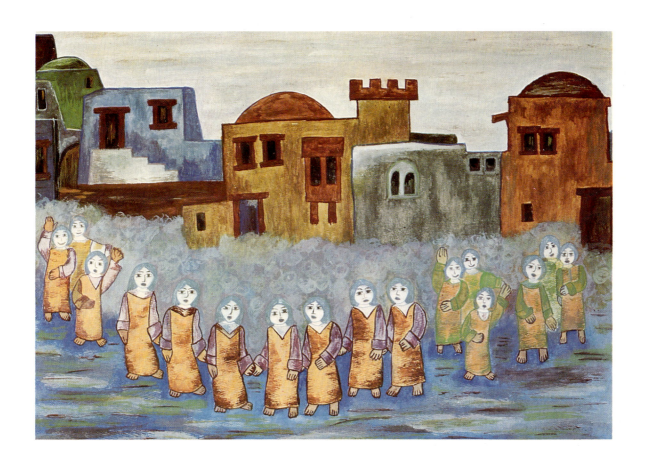

Martha Vizcaino Vargas, age 13, Ecuador

Group Work (Boys of Odakya Makoya), age 7-11, Japan

Anna Aroyo, age 12, England

Cornelia Luckener, age 12, West Germany

Susanna Bosneirth, age 13, Austria

● Mirre van den Ende, age 10, Holland

Elisabeth Bachmayer, age 10, Austria

Betty Campbell, age 11, U.S.A.

David Salomon & Cahbrera Espinoza, age 11, Ecuador

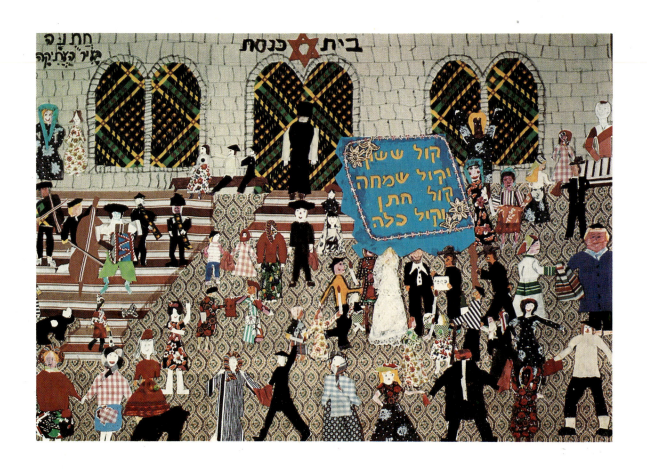

Group Work, age 11, England

Erik Hasselberg & Patrik Gustavsson, age 10, Sweden

Louise-Alison Canter, age 12, England

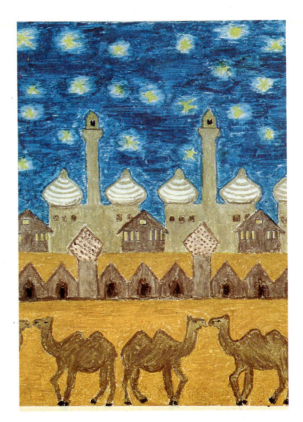

Amitai Harlev, age 10, Israel   Marco Canearolo, age 12, Italy

Aynat Bikel, age 12, Israel

Marcy Kamen, age 14, U.S.A.

Choi Hyun-Joo, age 10, South Korea

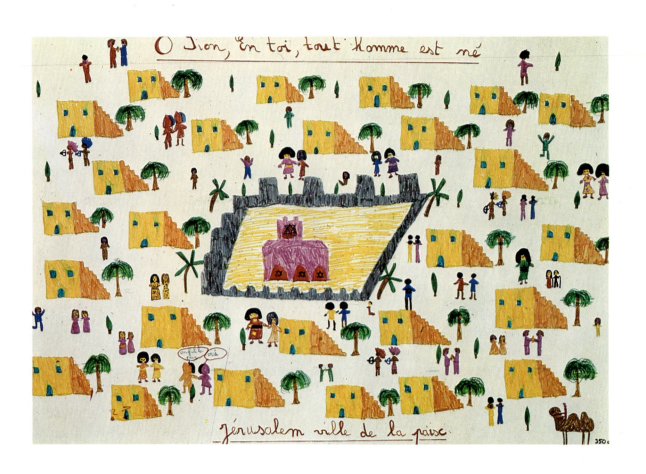

Anne-Marie Scotto, age 9½, France

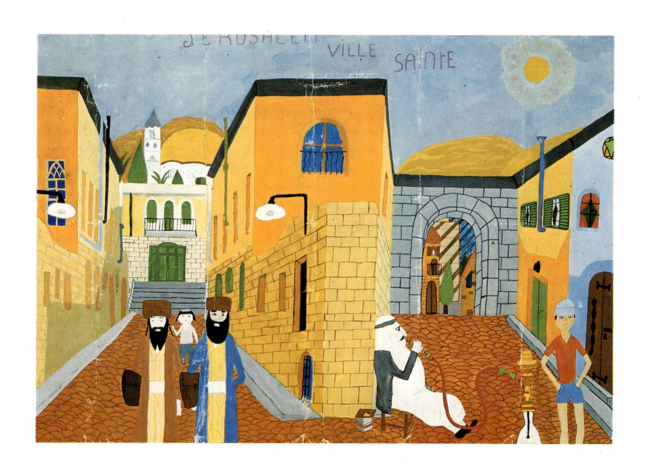

Beatrice Bitone, age 13, France

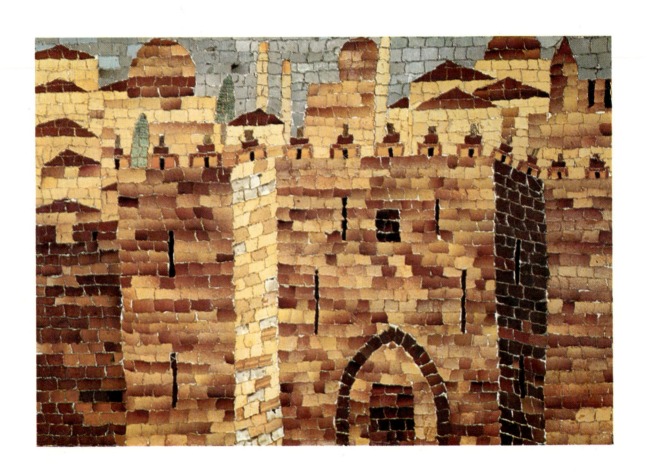

Lorette Goose, Belgium